GW01388337

An excellent book on fundamental Islamic information for children

Fundamental Teachings of Islam

(Part-I)

Presented by:

Majlis Madarasa-tul-Madinah and Majlis Al-Madina-tul-'Ilmiyyah

Translated into English by:

Majlis-e-Tarājim Dawat-e-Islami

Publisher:

Maktaba-tul-Madina Bab-ul-Madina, Karachi

اَلصَّلٰوةُ وَالسَّلَامُ عَلَيْكَ يَا رَسُوْلَ الله وَعَلٰى اٰلِكَ وَاَصْحٰبِكَ يَا حَبِيْبَ الله

Book name:

Fundamental Teachings of Islam (Part-I)

Jointly presented by:

Majlis Madrasa-tul-Madinah and Majlis Al-Madina-tul-'Ilmiyyah

Translated into English by:

Majlis Tarājim

Year of publication:

Jumādal Ukhrā 1434 AH, March, 2013

E.mail:

translation@dawateislami.net

Clarification

The **Urdu version** of the book 'Madanī Niṣāb for Madanī Qāidah' (published by Maktaba-tul-Madina) has been scrutinized by Majlis Taftīsh-e-Kutub-o-Rasāil (Dawat-e-Islami). Majlis Tarājim has translated the scrutinized Urdu version into English.

Contents at a Glance

A detailed table of contents can be seen at the end of the book.

Transliteration Chart

ء	A/a	ڑ	Ř/ř	ل	L/l
ا	A/a	ز	Z/z	م	M/m
ب	B/b	ژ	X/x	ن	N/n
پ	P/p	س	S/s	و	V/v, W/w
ت	T/t	ش	Sh/sh		
ٹ	Ṫ/ṫ	ص	Ṣ/ṣ	ہ / ہ / ۃ	Ĥ/ĥ
ث	Š/š	ض	Ḍ/ḍ	ی	Y/y
ج	J/j	ط	Ṭ/ṭ	ے	Y/y
چ	Ch	ظ	Ẓ/ẓ	َ	A/a
ح	Ḥ/ḥ	ع	‘	ُ	U/u
خ	Kh/kh	غ	Gh/gh	ِ	I/i
د	D/d	ف	F/f	و مدّہ	Ū/ū
ڈ	Ḋ/ḋ	ق	Q/q	ی مدّہ	Ī/ī
ذ	Ż/ż	ک	K/k	ا مدّہ	Ā/ā

اَلْحَمْدُ لِلّٰهِ رَبِّ الْعٰلَمِيْنَ وَالصَّلٰوةُ وَالسَّلَامُ عَلٰى سَيِّدِ الْمُرْسَلِيْنَ
اَمَّا بَعْدُ فَاَعُوْذُ بِاللّٰهِ مِنَ الشَّيْطٰنِ الرَّجِيْمِ ؕ بِسْمِ اللّٰهِ الرَّحْمٰنِ الرَّحِيْمِ ؕ

Al-Madīna-tul-'Ilmiyyaĥ

From: Shaykh-e-Ṭarīqat Amīr-e-Aĥl-e-Sunnat, founder of Dawat-e-Islami, 'Allāmaĥ Maulānā Abu Bilal **Muhammad Ilyas Attar Qadiri** Razavi Ziyai دَامَتْ بَرَكَاتُهُمُ الْعَالِيَه.

اَلْحَمْدُ لِلّٰهِ عَلٰى اِحْسَانِهٖ وَ بِفَضْلِ رَسُوْلِهٖ صَلَّى اللهُ تَعَالٰى عَلَيْهِ وَاٰلِهٖ وَسَلَّم

Dawat-e-Islami, a global and non-political movement for the preaching of Quran and Sunnaĥ, is determined to revive Sunnaĥ and spread righteousness as well as the knowledge of Sharī'aĥ throughout the world. In order to carry out these great and significant tasks in an excellent way, several Majālis (departments) have been formed including the Majlis 'Al-Madīna-tul-'Ilmiyyaĥ' which consists of the 'Ulamā and Muftis of Dawat-e-Islami. This Majlis has ambitiously taken on the responsibility of serving religion in the areas of knowledge, research and publication. It has the following six departments:

- Department of books of A'lā Ḥaḍrat رَحْمَةُ اللهِ تَعَالٰى عَلَيْه.
- Department of teaching books.
- Department of reforming books.
- Department of translation.
- Department of scrutiny of books.
- Department of referencing and documentation.

The topmost priority of Al-Madīna-tul-'Ilmiyyaĥ is to present the precious books of A'lā Ḥaḍrat, Imām-e-Aĥl-e-Sunnat, reviver of Sunnaĥ, eradicator of Bid'aĥ, scholar of Sharī'aĥ, 'Allāmaĥ Maulānā Al-Ḥāj, Al-Qārī, Ash-Shāĥ Imām Aḥmad Razā Khān عَلَيْهِ رَحْمَةُ الرَّحْمٰن in an easily understandable way according to the needs of the present age.

All the Islamic brothers and sisters should whole-heartedly cooperate in the development of the Madanī work of knowledge, research and publication, and study every book published by the Majlis as well as persuading others to do the same.

May all the Majālis of Dawat-e-Islami including Al-Madīna-tul-'Ilmiyyaĥ progress by leaps and bounds! May Allah عَزَّوَجَلَّ bestow success upon us in our worldly life as well in the afterlife by enabling us to perform each and every good deed with sincerity! May we all be blessed with martyrdom under the green dome, burial in Jannat-ul-Baqī' and an abode in Jannat-ul-Firdaus.

آمِین بِجَاہِ النَّبِیِّ الْاَمِین صَلَّی اللّٰہُ تَعَالٰی عَلَیْہِ وَاٰلِہٖ وَسَلَّم

Translated into English by:

Majlis Tarājim

Praise and Privilege

Sayyidunā Imām 'Abdullāĥ Bin 'Umar Bayḍāwī عَلَیْہِ رَحْمَۃُ اللّٰہِ الْقَوِی (who had passed away in 685 A.H.) stated, 'The one who obeys Allah عَزَّوَجَلَّ and His Beloved Prophet صَلَّی اللّٰہُ تَعَالٰی عَلَیْہِ وَاٰلِہٖ وَسَلَّم, is praised in the world and will be privileged in the Hereafter.' *(Tafsīr Baghwī, Part 22, Sūraĥ Al-Ḥazāb, Taḥat-ul-Āyaĥ 71, Verse 4, p. 388)*

Preface

The Holy Quran is the last book of Allah عَزَّوَجَلَّ. The one reciting and acting upon it succeeds in his worldly life as well as in afterlife. اَلْحَمْدُلِلّٰه عَزَّوَجَلَّ! Dawat-e-Islami, a global and non-political movement for the preaching of Quran and Sunnaĥ, has established countless Madāris [Islamic institutions] namely Madrasa-tul-Madīnaĥ for Ḥifẓ [memorizing the Quran by heart] and Nāẓiraĥ [reciting the Quran by looking at it] within and outside Pakistan. By the time of the writing of this preface, about 75,000 children are acquiring free education of Ḥifẓ and Nāẓiraĥ in Pakistan alone. In these Madāris, emphasis is placed on Islamic education and upbringing of children besides the learning of the Holy Quran so that the students completing education from Madrasa-tul-Madīnaĥ would have Islamic knowledge in addition to the ability of reciting the Holy Quran correctly, and so that they would emerge in society as knowledgeable, practicing, decent and well-mannered Muslims who are free from evils, able enough to distinguish between right and wrong and zealous in striving to reform themselves and the people of the entire world.

As the children enrolled in Qāidaĥ classes are at their early ages, this book has been designed in view of their intellectual capacity, covering basic religious topics including تَعَوُّذ (Ta'awwuż), تَسْمِيَه (Tasmiyyaĥ), ثَنَاء (Šanā), short and easy Du'ās, basic beliefs, essential rulings, knowledge about divine books, initial information about Prophets عَلَيْهِمُ السَّلَام, blessed companions رَضِىَ اللّٰهُ تَعَالٰى عَنْهُم and Auliyā of Allah.

The presentation of 'Fundamental Teachings of Islam (Part-I)' is a joint effort of Madrasa-tul-Madīnaĥ and Al-Madīna-tul-'Ilmiyyaĥ, whereas its Shar'ī scrutiny has been carried out by Dar-ul-Iftā Aĥl-e-Sunnat.

Yiĥī ĥay ārzū Ta'līm-e-Quran 'ām ĥo jāye
Ĥar aik parcham say aūnchā parcham Islam ĥo jāye

May the teachings of Quran all over the world spread
May the flag of Islam flies higher than all other flags

Majlis Madrasa-tul-Madinaĥ and Majlis Al-Madina-tul-'Ilmiyyaĥ
Translated into English by: Majlis Tarājim

Hamd Bari Ta'ala

Tū ĥī Mālik-e-baḥr-o-bar ĥay Yā Allahu Yā Allah
Tū ĥī Khāliq-e-jinn-o-bashar ĥay Yā Allahu Yā Allah

Tū Abadī ĥay Tū Azalī ĥay Tayrā nām 'Alīm-o-'Alī ĥay
Żāt Tayrī sab say bar-tar ĥay Yā Allahu Yā Allah

Waṣf bayān kartay ĥayn sāray sang-o-shajar aur chānd sitāray
Tasbīḥ ĥar khushk-o-tar ĥay Yā Allahu Yā Allah

Tayrā charchā galī galī ĥay ḋālī ḋālī kalī kalī ĥay
Wāṣif ĥar aīk pĥūl-o-šamar ĥay Yā Allahu Yā Allah

Khalqat jab pānī ko tar-say rim jĥim rim jĥim barkĥā bar-say
Ĥar aīk par Raḥmat kī naẓar ĥay Yā Allahu Yā Allah

Rāt nay jab sar apnā cĥupāyā chiřyaun nay yeĥ żikr sunāyā
Naghmaĥ bār nasīm-e-saḥar ĥay Yā Allahu Yā Allah

Bakhsh day Tū 'Aṭṭār ko Maulā wāsiṭaĥ Tujĥ ko us piyāray kā
Jo kaĥ Nabiyaun kā Sarwar ĥay Yā Allahu Yā Allah

(Wasāil-e-Bakhshish, pp. 42)

Na’at-e-Mustafa ﷺ

Ānkĥaun kā tārā nām-e-Muhammad
Dil kā ujālā nām-e-Muhammad

Dawlat jo chāĥo dauno jaĥān kī
Kar lo waẓīfaĥ nām-e-Muhammad

Nūḥ-o-Khalīl-o-Mūsā-o-‘Īsā
Sab kā ĥay Āqā nām-e-Muhammad

Pāyaīn murādayn dauno jaĥān mayn
Jis nay pukārā nām-e-Muhammad

Pūcĥay gā Maulā layā ĥay kyā kyā
Mayn yeĥ kaĥūn gā nām-e-Muhammad

Apnay Razā kay qurbān jāon
Jis nay sikĥāyā nām-e-Muhammad

Apnay Jamīl Rizwī kay dil mayn
Ājā samā jā nām-e-Muhammad

(Maddaḥ-e-Ḥabīb Shaykh Maulānā
Jamīl-ur-Raḥmān Raḍavī عَلَیۡہِ رَحۡمَۃُ اللّٰہِ الۡقَوِی*)*

Aẓkār

Ṣalāĥ

Šanā

سُبْحٰنَكَ اللّٰهُمَّ وَبِحَمْدِكَ

وَتَبَارَكَ اسْمُكَ وَتَعَالٰى جَدُّكَ وَلَآ اِلٰهَ غَيْرُكَ ط

Translation:

Glory to You, Yā Allah! I praise You, Your name is Blessed;
greatness and glory to You in the highest and none is worthy of worship except You.

Ta'awwuż

اَعُوْذُ بِاللّٰهِ مِنَ الشَّيْطٰنِ الرَّجِيْمِ ط

Translation:

I seek refuge by Allah from Satan, the accursed.

Tasmiyyaĥ

بِسْمِ اللّٰهِ الرَّحْمٰنِ الرَّحِيْمِ ط

Translation:

Allah's name I begin with, the Most Kind, the Most Merciful.

Kalimāt (Statements of Faith)

Kalimah Ṭayyibah

لَآ اِلٰهَ اِلَّا اللّٰهُ مُحَمَّدٌ رَّسُوْلُ اللّٰهِ ؕ

Translation:

There is none worthy of worship
except Allah, Muhammad is the Prophet of Allah.

Kalimah Shahādat

اَشْهَدُ اَنْ لَّآ اِلٰهَ اِلَّا اللّٰهُ وَحْدَهٗ لَا شَرِيْكَ لَهٗ وَاَشْهَدُ اَنَّ مُحَمَّدًا عَبْدُهٗ وَرَسُوْلُهٗ ؕ

Translation:

I testify that there is none worthy of worship except Allah. He is alone and He has no partner and I testify that Muhammad is His (Distinguished) Servant and His Prophet.

Kalimah Tamjīd

سُبْحَانَ اللّٰهِ وَالْحَمْدُ لِلّٰهِ وَلَآ اِلٰهَ
اِلَّا اللّٰهُ وَاللّٰهُ اَكْبَرُ ؕ وَلَا حَوْلَ وَلَا قُوَّةَ اِلَّا بِاللّٰهِ الْعَلِيِّ الْعَظِيْمِ ؕ

Translation:

Glory be to Allah and all praise be to Allah and there is none worthy of worship except Allah, and Allah is Great and there is no power to keep away from sins and no ability to do good but from Allah who is the greatest.

Ṣalat-'Alan-Nabī ﷺ

The Holy Prophet صَلَّى اللهُ تَعَالٰى عَلَيْهِ وَاٰلِهٖ وَسَلَّم has stated, 'Wherever you are, recite Ṣalāt upon me as your Ṣalāt reaches me.' *(Sunan Abī Dāwūd, Kitāb-ul-Manāsik, Bāb: Ziyārat-il-Qubūr, Vol. 2, p. 315, Ḥadīš 2042)*

صَلُّوْا عَلَى الْحَبِيْب   صَلَّى اللّٰهُ تَعَالٰى عَلٰى مُحَمَّد

اَلصَّلٰوةُ وَالسَّلَامُ عَلَيْكَ يَا رَسُوْلَ الله

May Ṣalāt and Salām be to you, O Rasul of Allah

اَلصَّلٰوةُ وَالسَّلَامُ عَلَيْكَ يَا نَبِيَّ الله

May Ṣalāt and Salām be to you, O Prophet of Allah

وَعَلٰى اٰلِكَ وَاَصْحٰبِكَ يَا حَبِيْبَ الله

And to your descendants and your companions, O Beloved of Allah

وَعَلٰى اٰلِكَ وَاَصْحٰبِكَ يَا نُوْرَ الله

And to your descendants and companions, O Nūr of Allah

Du'as

Du'a before Quranic recitation

أَعُوذُ بِاللّٰهِ مِنَ الشَّيْطٰنِ الرَّجِيْمِ ط

Translation:

I seek refuge by Allah from Satan, the accursed.

Du'ā to be recited when moving to a higher place

اَللّٰهُ اَكْبَرُ ط

Translation:

Allah is the Greatest.

Du'ā to be recited when moving from higher to lower place

سُبْحٰنَ اللّٰه ط

Translation:

Glory be to Allah.

Du'a to be recited before drinking water

بِسْمِ اللّٰهِ الرَّحْمٰنِ الرَّحِيْمِ ط

Translation:

Allah's name I begin with,
the Most Kind, the Most Merciful.

Du'a to be recited after drinking water

اَلْحَمْدُ لِلّٰهِ رَبِّ الْعٰلَمِيْنَ ط

Translation:

All praise to Allah, Rab of the worlds.

Du'a to be recited before eating food

بِسْمِ اللّٰهِ وَعَلٰى بَرَكَةِ اللّٰهِ ط

Translation:

Allah's name I begin with,
and with the bounty of Allah I eat.

Du'a to be recited after eating food

اَلْحَمْدُ لِلّٰهِ الَّذِيْ اَطْعَمَنَا وَسَقَانَا وَجَعَلَنَا مُسْلِمِيْنَ ط

Translation:

I express gratitude to Almighty Allah who has made us eat and drink and has made us Muslims.

(Sunan Abī Dāwūd, Kitāb-ul-Aṭ'imaĥ, Vol. 3, p. 513, Ḥadiš 3850)

Du'a to be recited before going to sleep

اَللّٰهُمَّ بِاسْمِكَ اَمُوْتُ وَاَحْيَا ط

Translation:

O Allah! With Your name I die and get resurrected
(i.e. sleep and wake).

(Ṣaḥīḥ Bukhārī, Kitāb-ud-Da'wat, vol. 4, pp. 193, Ḥadīš 6314)

Du'ā to be recited after awakening from sleep

اَلْحَمْدُ لِلّٰهِ الَّذِیْۤ اَحْیَانَا بَعْدَ مَاۤ اَمَاتَنَا وَاِلَیْهِ النُّشُوْرُ ط

Translation:

All praise to Allah عَزَّوَجَلَّ who has revived (awakened) us after death (sleep), and we are to return towards Him.

(Al-Marja'-us-Sabiq)

Du'ā to be recited when meeting a Muslim

اَلسَّلَامُ عَلَیْکُمْ وَرَحْمَةُ اللّٰهِ وَبَرَکَاتُه ط

Translation:

Peace be upon you,
and also the bounty and blessing of Allah.

Du'a to be recited when shaking hands with others

یَغْفِرُ اللّٰهُ لَنَا وَلَکُمْ ط

Translation:

May Allah forgive you and me.

Du'a of Gratification

جَزَاکَ اللّٰهُ خَیْرًا ط

Translation:

May Allah give you better reward.

Beliefs

Faith and types of its descriptions

Question 1: What is faith?

Answer: To believe in all commandments and teachings Prophet Muhammad صَلَّى اللهُ تَعَالٰى عَلَيْهِ وَاٰلِهٖ وَسَلَّم has brought from Allah عَزَّوَجَلَّ and to accept all of them whole-heartedly is called faith.

Question 2: What are the types of the descriptions of faith? Describe them.

Answer: There are 2 types of the descriptions of faith:

(1) Īmān-e-Mujmal (2) Īmān-e-Mufaṣṣal

Question 3: What is 'Īmān-e-Mujmal'?

Answer: A brief description of faith is called 'Īmān-e-Mujmal'.

Question 4: Recite aloud Īmān-e-Mujmal with its translation.

Answer:

Īmān-e-Mujmal

اٰمَنْتُ بِاللهِ كَمَا هُوَ بِاَسْمَآئِهٖ

وَصِفَاتِهٖ وَقَبِلْتُ جَمِيْعَ اَحْكَامِهٖ اِقْرَارٌۢ بِاللِّسَانِ وَ تَصْدِيْقٌۢ بِالْقَلْبِ ط

Translation:

I solemnly declare my belief in Allah as He is with all His names and attributes, and I have accepted (to obey) all His commandments by pledging with my tongue and testifying them with my heart.

Question 5: What is Īmān-e-Mufaṣṣal?

Answer: A detailed description of faith is called 'Īmān-e-Mufaṣṣal'.

Question 6: Recite aloud Īmān-e-Mufaṣṣal with its translation.

Answer:

Īmān-e-Mufaṣṣal

اٰمَنْتُ بِاللّٰهِ وَمَلٰٓئِكَتِهٖ وَكُتُبِهٖ وَرُسُلِهٖ
وَالْيَوْمِ الْاٰخِرِ وَالْقَدْرِ خَيْرِهٖ وَشَرِّهٖ مِنَ اللّٰهِ تَعَالٰى وَالْبَعْثِ بَعْدَ الْمَوْتِ ط

I believe in Allah, His Angels, His (revealed) Books, His Prophets, the Day of Judgment and (I believe that) good and bad destiny is from Allah and (I believe that) there will be resurrection after death.

Five before five

Dear children! Certainly, life is very short. The time we have once spent will never come back, and any hope of having time in future is deception as we do not know what would happen to us in future. Perhaps we may have met our death the next moment. The Beloved and Blessed Prophet صَلَّى اللهُ تَعَالٰى عَلَيْهِ وَاٰلِهٖ وَسَلَّم has stated, 'Value five things before five things: (1) Youth before old age (2) Health before illness (3) Wealth before deprivation (4) Leisure before busyness [i.e. being busy]. (5) Life before death.' *(Al-Mustadrak, vol. 5, pp. 435, Ḥadīš 7912, Dar-ul-Ma'rifaĥ, Beirut)*

Allah عَزَّوَجَلَّ

Question 1: Who has created us?

Answer: Allah عَزَّوَجَلَّ has created us.

Question 2: Who has created the earth, the sky, the sun, the moon and the stars?

Answer: The earth, the sky, the sun, the moon and the stars have all been created by Allah عَزَّوَجَلَّ.

Question 3: Who do we worship?

Answer: We worship Allah عَزَّوَجَلَّ.

Question 4: Who listens to and sees everything?

Answer: Allah عَزَّوَجَلَّ listens to and sees everything.

Question 5: Can anything be hidden from Allah عَزَّوَجَلَّ?

Answer: No! Nothing can be hidden from Allah عَزَّوَجَلَّ. He knows everything.

Our Beloved Prophet ﷺ

Question 1: What is the blessed name of our Beloved Prophet صَلَّى اللهُ تَعَالٰى عَلَيْهِ وَاٰلِهٖ وَسَلَّم?

Answer: The blessed name of our Beloved Prophet صَلَّى اللهُ تَعَالٰى عَلَيْهِ وَاٰلِهٖ وَسَلَّم is Muhammad صَلَّى اللهُ تَعَالٰى عَلَيْهِ وَاٰلِهٖ وَسَلَّم.

Question 2: In which city did the blessed birth of our Beloved Prophet صَلَّى اللهُ تَعَالٰى عَلَيْهِ وَاٰلِهٖ وَسَلَّم take place?

Answer: The blessed birth of our Beloved Prophet صَلَّى اللهُ تَعَالٰى عَلَيْهِ وَاٰلِهٖ وَسَلَّم took place in Makka-tul-Mukarramaĥ, a famous city of Arabia.

Question 3: What is the date and month of the birth of our Beloved Prophet صَلَّى اللهُ تَعَالٰى عَلَيْهِ وَاٰلِهٖ وَسَلَّم?

Answer: The blessed birth of our Beloved Prophet صَلَّى اللهُ تَعَالٰى عَلَيْهِ وَاٰلِهٖ وَسَلَّم took place on 12th Rabī'-ul-Awwal.

Question 4: On which day was our Beloved Prophet صَلَّى اللهُ تَعَالٰى عَلَيْهِ وَاٰلِهٖ وَسَلَّم born?

Answer: Our Beloved Prophet صَلَّى اللهُ تَعَالٰى عَلَيْهِ وَاٰلِهٖ وَسَلَّم was born on a Monday.

Question 5: What is the name of the father of our Beloved Prophet صَلَّى اللّٰهُ تَعَالٰى عَلَيْهِ وَاٰلِهٖ وَسَلَّم?

Answer: The name of the father of our Beloved Prophet صَلَّى اللّٰهُ تَعَالٰى عَلَيْهِ وَاٰلِهٖ وَسَلَّم is Sayyidunā 'Abdullāĥ رَضِيَ اللّٰهُ تَعَالٰى عَنْهُ.

Question 6: What is the name of the mother of our Beloved Prophet صَلَّى اللّٰهُ تَعَالٰى عَلَيْهِ وَاٰلِهٖ وَسَلَّم?

Answer: The name of the mother of our Beloved Prophet صَلَّى اللّٰهُ تَعَالٰى عَلَيْهِ وَاٰلِهٖ وَسَلَّم is Sayyidatunā Āminaĥ رَضِيَ اللّٰهُ تَعَالٰى عَنْهَا.

Question 7: Where is the blessed tomb of our Beloved Prophet صَلَّى اللّٰهُ تَعَالٰى عَلَيْهِ وَاٰلِهٖ وَسَلَّم situated?

Answer: The blessed tomb of our Beloved Prophet صَلَّى اللّٰهُ تَعَالٰى عَلَيْهِ وَاٰلِهٖ وَسَلَّم is situated in Madīna-tul-Munawwaraĥ.

Question 8: What was the age of our Beloved Prophet صَلَّى اللّٰهُ تَعَالٰى عَلَيْهِ وَاٰلِهٖ وَسَلَّم?

Answer: The age of our Beloved Prophet صَلَّى اللّٰهُ تَعَالٰى عَلَيْهِ وَاٰلِهٖ وَسَلَّم was 63 years.

Our Religion

Question 1: Who are we by religion?

Answer: We are Muslim by religion.

Question 2: What is our religion?

Answer: Our religion is Islam.

Question 3: Who is a Muslim?

Answer: One who believes in Islam is a Muslim.

Question 4: Who do the Muslims worship?

Answer: The Muslims worship Allah عَزَّوَجَلَّ only.

Question 5: What does Islam teach us?

Answer: Islam teaches us truthfulness, neatness, goodness and righteousness.

Question 6: What is the Kalimaĥ [i.e. creed] of Islam?

Answer: The Kalimaĥ [i.e. creed] of Islam is:

لَآ اِلٰهَ اِلَّا اللّٰهُ مُحَمَّدٌ رَّسُوْلُ اللّٰهِ ؕ

There is none worthy of worship except Allah, and Muhammad is the Prophet of Allah.

Pillars of Islam

Question 1: How many pillars of Islam are there?

Answer: There are five pillars of Islam: (1) To testify that there is no one worthy to be worshipped except Allah عَزَّوَجَلَّ, and Muhammad صَلَّى اللهُ تَعَالٰى عَلَيْهِ وَاٰلِهٖ وَسَلَّم is a distinguished Servant and Prophet of Allah عَزَّوَجَلَّ. (2) To offer Ṣalāĥ (3) To pay Zakāĥ (4) To perform Hajj (5) To keep fasts in Ramaḍān.
(Ṣaḥīḥ Bukhārī, Kitāb-ul-Īmān, Vol. 1, p. 14, Ḥadīš 8)

Question 2: How many Ṣalāĥs are Farḍ (obligatory) in a day and night?

Answer: Five Ṣalāĥs are Farḍ (obligatory) in a day and night.

Question 3: Tell the name of the five Farḍ Ṣalāĥs.

Answer: (1) Fajr (2) Ẓuĥr (3) ʻAṣr (4) Maghrib (5) ʻIshā

Question 4: In which month is it Farḍ for the Muslims to keep fasts?

Answer: It is Farḍ for the Muslims to keep fasts in the blessed month of Ramadan.

Question 5: For whom is Hajj Farḍ?

Answer: Hajj is Farḍ once, in lifetime, for every such Muslim who is capable of performing it.

Question 6: Where is Hajj performed?

Answer: Hajj is performed in Makka-tul-Mukarramaĥ.

The Angels

Question 1: Who are the angels?

Answer: The angels are a creation of Allah عَزَّوَجَلَّ and are created from Nūr (light).

Question 2: What do the angels do?

Answer: The angels do exactly what Allah عَزَّوَجَلَّ orders them.

Question 3: Who is the chief of the angels?

Answer: The chief of the angels is Jibrīl عَلَيْهِ السَّلَام.

Question 4: What is the total number of the angels?

Answer: Only Allah عَزَّوَجَلَّ and His Prophet صَلَّى اللّٰهُ تَعَالٰى عَلَيْهِ وَاٰلِهٖ وَسَلَّم better know the total number of the angels.

Question 5: What do the angels eat and drink?

Answer: The angels do not eat and drink anything.

Paradise under the feet of mother

Sayyidunā Anas Bin Mālik رَضِىَ اللّٰهُ تَعَالٰى عَنْهُ has narrated that the Prophet of mankind, the Peace of our heart and mind, the most Generous and Kind صَلَّى اللّٰهُ تَعَالٰى عَلَيْهِ وَاٰلِهٖ وَسَلَّم has stated, 'Paradise lies under the feet of mothers.' *(Kanz-ul-'Ummāl, Kitāb-un-Nikah, Vol. 16, p. 192, Ḥadīš 45431)*

The Prophets عَلَيۡهِمُ الصَّلٰوةُ وَالسَّلَام

Question 1: Who is called a Prophet?

Answer: The human to whom Allah عَزَّوَجَلَّ has sent revelation for guidance is called a Prophet.

Question 2: Which Prophet عَلَيۡهِ السَّلَام did Allah عَزَّوَجَلَّ create first?

Answer: Allah عَزَّوَجَلَّ created Sayyidunā Ādam عَلَيۡهِ السَّلَام first.

Question 3: Who is the last Prophet sent in the world?

Answer: The last Prophet sent in the world is our Beloved Prophet Muhammad Mustafa صَلَّى اللهُ تَعَالٰى عَلَيۡهِ وَاٰلِهٖ وَسَلَّم.

Question 4: After our Beloved Prophet صَلَّى اللهُ تَعَالٰى عَلَيۡهِ وَاٰلِهٖ وَسَلَّم, can any Prophet come in the world?

Answer: No Prophet can come in the world after our Beloved Prophet صَلَّى اللهُ تَعَالٰى عَلَيۡهِ وَاٰلِهٖ وَسَلَّم.

Question 5: If anyone makes a false claim of Prophethood, what is he called?

Answer: If someone makes a false claim of Prophethood, he is called a 'Każżāb (biggest liar)'.

Question 6: Are all the Prophets عَلَيْهِمُ الصَّلٰوةُ وَالسَّلَام alive in their graves?

Answer: Yes!

Question 7: Who is the chief of all the Prophets عَلَيْهِمُ السَّلَام?

Answer: The chief of all the Prophets is our Beloved Prophet Muhammad Mustafa صَلَّى اللّٰهُ تَعَالٰى عَلَيْهِ وَاٰلِهٖ وَسَلَّم.

Question 8: What meaning of the word 'Prophet' has A'lā Ḥaḍrat رَحْمَةُ اللّٰهِ تَعَالٰى عَلَيْه stated in Kanz-ul-Īmān?

Answer: 'The one who gives the news of Ghayb.'

Question 9: Tell the names of some of the Prophets عَلَيْهِمُ الصَّلٰوةُ وَالسَّلَام.

Answer:

1. Sayyidunā Adam عَلَيْهِ السَّلَام
2. Sayyidunā Mūsā عَلَيْهِ السَّلَام
3. Sayyidunā Dāwūd عَلَيْهِ السَّلَام
4. Sayyidunā Nūḥ عَلَيْهِ السَّلَام
5. Sayyidunā 'Īsā عَلَيْهِ السَّلَام
6. Sayyidunā Sulaymān عَلَيْهِ السَّلَام
7. Our Beloved Prophet Muhammad Mustafa صَلَّى اللّٰهُ تَعَالٰى عَلَيْهِ وَاٰلِهٖ وَسَلَّم.

Mu'jizāt of Prophets عَلَيۡهِمُ الصَّلٰوةُ وَالسَّلَام

Question 1: What is a Mu'jizaĥ?

Answer: A supernatural act performed by a Prophet after he has made the proclamation of his Prophethood is called a Mu'jizaĥ.

Question 2: Which is the Prophet عَلَيۡهِ السَّلَام who would turn iron soft like wax when he took it in his hand?

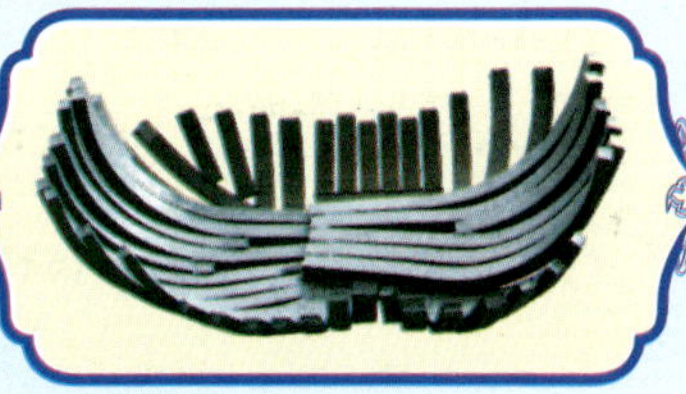

Answer: When Sayyidunā Dāwūd عَلَيۡهِ السَّلَام took iron in his hand, it would become soft like wax.

Question 3: Which is the Prophet عَلَيۡهِ السَّلَام who made a passage through a river by hitting his staff (i.e. stick) over the river water?

Answer: Sayyidunā Mūsā عَلَيۡهِ السَّلَام made a passage through a river by hitting his staff over the river water.

Question 4: Which is the Prophet who smiled to have heard the sound of an ant from 3 miles?

Answer: Sayyidunā Sulaymān عَلَيۡهِ السَّلَام smiled to have heard the sound of an ant from 3 miles.

Question 5: Which Prophet had the she-camel of Paradise that would drink all the water of the pond on its turn?

Answer: Sayyidunā Ṣāliḥ عَلَيۡهِ السَّلَام had the she-camel of Paradise that would drink all the water of the pond on its turn.

The Revealed Books

Question 1: Which books are called the revealed books?

Answer: The books revealed by Allah عَزَّوَجَلَّ are called the revealed books.

Question 2: Whom were these books revealed to?

Answer: These books were revealed to the Prophets عَلَيْهِمُ الصَّلٰوةُ وَالسَّلَام.

Question 3: Why were these books revealed?

Answer: These books were revealed for the guidance of mankind.

Question 4: Which are the famous revealed books?

Answer:

1. The Tawrāt
2. The Zabūr
3. The Injīl
4. The Holy Quran

A prominent quality of Islam

Great importance has been attached to modesty in Islam. It is stated in a Ḥadīš, 'Verily, every religion has a quality and the quality of Islam is modesty.' *(Sunan Ibn Mājaĥ, Vol. 4, p. 460, Ḥadīš 4181; Dār-ul-Ma'rifaĥ, Beirut)* In other words, every Ummaĥ has one such quality that is more prominent than its other qualities, and that prominent quality of Islam is modesty

The Companions رَضِیَ اللہُ تَعَالٰی عَنْہُم

Question 1: Who is called a companion (a Ṣaḥābī)?

Answer: A companion is the one who, in the state of Īmān, saw the Beloved and Blessed Prophet صَلَّی اللہُ تَعَالٰی عَلَیْہِ وَاٰلِہٖ وَسَلَّم and who passed away in the state of Īmān.

Question 2: Which companions are referred to as Khulafā-e-Rāshidīn?

Answer: The four blessed companions who became the first four caliphs of the Muslims after the apparent demise of the Holy Prophet صَلَّی اللہُ تَعَالٰی عَلَیْہِ وَاٰلِہٖ وَسَلَّم are known as the Khulafā-e-Rāshidīn.

Question 3: Tell the names of the Khulafā-e-Rāshidīn.

Answer:

- Amīr-ul-Mūminīn Sayyidunā Abū Bakr Ṣiddīq رَضِیَ اللہُ تَعَالٰی عَنْہُ.
- Amīr-ul-Mūminīn Sayyidunā 'Umar Fārūq A'ẓam رَضِیَ اللہُ تَعَالٰی عَنْہُ.
- Amīr-ul-Mūminīn Sayyidunā 'Ušmān Ghanī رَضِیَ اللہُ تَعَالٰی عَنْہُ.
- Amīr-ul-Mūminīn Sayyidunā 'Alī Murtaḍā رَضِیَ اللہُ تَعَالٰی عَنْہُ.

Question 4: Tell the names of some other companions of the Holy Prophet صَلَّى اللّٰهُ تَعَالٰى عَلَيْهِ وَاٰلِهٖ وَسَلَّم.

Answer: The names of some other companions of the Holy Prophet صَلَّى اللّٰهُ تَعَالٰى عَلَيْهِ وَاٰلِهٖ وَسَلَّم include:

- Sayyidunā 'Abdullāĥ Bin 'Abbās رَضِىَ اللّٰهُ تَعَالٰى عَنْهُمَا.
- Sayyidunā 'Abdullāĥ Bin 'Umar رَضِىَ اللّٰهُ تَعَالٰى عَنْهُمَا
- Sayyidunā 'Abdullāĥ Bin Mas'ūd رَضِىَ اللّٰهُ تَعَالٰى عَنْه
- Sayyidunā Amīr Mu'āwiyaĥ رَضِىَ اللّٰهُ تَعَالٰى عَنْه
- Sayyidunā Imām Ḥasan رَضِىَ اللّٰهُ تَعَالٰى عَنْه
- Sayyidunā Imām Ḥusaīn رَضِىَ اللّٰهُ تَعَالٰى عَنْه

Plant a tree in Paradise

Dear children! You can realize the importance of time by the fact that whilst living in the world you can have a tree planted for you in Paradise within a second! To have a tree planted in Paradise is very easy. According to a Ḥadīš stated in Ibn Mājaĥ, 'A tree will be planted in Paradise for the one who recites any of these four phrases: (1) سُبْحٰنَ اللّٰهِ (2) اَلْحَمْدُ لِلّٰهِ (3) لَآ اِلٰهَ اِلَّا اللّٰهُ (4) اَللّٰهُ اَكْبَر'

(Sunan Ibn-e-Mājaĥ, Vol. 4, p. 252, Ḥadīš 3807, Dār-ul-Ma'rifaĥ, Beirut)

Auliyā Allah رَحِمَهُمُ اللّٰهُ السَّلَام

Question 1: Who is called a Walīyullāĥ (friend of Allah عَزَّوَجَلَّ)?

Answer: The Muslim who gives up his desires in devotion to Allah عَزَّوَجَلَّ and His Prophet صَلَّى اللهُ تَعَالٰى عَلَيْهِ وَاٰلِهٖ وَسَلَّم , and always obeys them is called a Walīyullāĥ.

Question 2: Tell the names of some Auliyā Allah رَحِمَهُمُ الله and also tell where are their shrines situated?

Answer: In relation to the 8 doors of Paradise, here are the names of 8 Auliyā Allah with the names of the cities where their shrines are situated.

- Sayyidunā Shaykh 'Abdul Qādir Jīlānī (Ghauš-e-A'ẓam رَحْمَةُ اللهِ تَعَالٰى عَلَيْه): His shrine is situated in Baghdad, Iraq.
- Sayyidunā Mu'īnuddīn Chishtī رَحْمَةُ اللهِ تَعَالٰى عَلَيْه: His shrine is situated in Ajmer, India.
- Sayyidunā Shaykh Shaĥābuddīn Suĥarwardī رَحْمَةُ اللهِ تَعَالٰى عَلَيْه: His shrine is situated in Suhrward, Iran.

- Sayyidunā Shaykh Baĥāuddīn Naqshband رحمۃ اللہ تعالی علیہ: His shrine is situated in Bukhara, Russia.
- Sayyidunā 'Alī Ĥajwairī (Dātā Ganj Bakhsh) رحمۃ اللہ تعالی علیہ: His shrine is situated in Markaz-ul-Auliyā Lahore, Pakistan.
- Sayyidunā Baĥāuddīn Zikriyaĥ Multānī رحمۃ اللہ تعالی علیہ: His shrine is situated in Madina-tul-Auliyā Multan, Pakistan.
- Sayyidunā Bābā Farīduddīn Ganj Shakar رحمۃ اللہ تعالی علیہ: His shrine is situated in Pakpattan, Pakistan.
- Sayyidunā Imām Aĥl-e-Sunnat Maulana Shah Imām Ahmad Razā Khān علیہ رحمۃ الرحمٰن: His shrine is situated in Bareilly, India.

Cleanliness

The Holy Prophet صلی اللہ تعالی علیہ والہ وسلم has stated: Cleanliness is half faith.

(Ṣaḥīḥ Muslim, Kitāb-ut-Ṭaĥārat, p. 140, Ḥadīš 223)

Acts of Worship

Wuḍū

Question 1: What and how many Farāiḍ (obligations) are there in Wuḍū?

Answer: There are four Farāiḍ in Wuḍū:

1. To wash the face.
2. To wash both forearms up to the elbows.
3. To pass a wet hand over one fourth part of the head.
4. To wash both feet up to the ankles. *(Namāz key Aḥkām, p. 14)*

Question 2: What should we recite before we make Wuḍū?

Answer: It is a Sunnaĥ to recite بِسْمِ اللهِ الرَّحْمٰنِ الرَّحِيْمِ before making Wuḍū.

Question 3: What is the excellence of reciting بِسۡمِ اللّٰه before making Wuḍū?

Answer: If a person recites بِسۡمِ اللّٰهِ وَالۡحَمۡدُ لِلّٰه before he makes Wuḍū, the angels will keep on writing virtues for him for as long as his Wuḍū exists. *(Mu'jam-ul-Zawāid, Kitāb-ut-Ṭahārat, Vol. 1, p. 513, Ḥadīš 112)*

Question 4: What is the excellence of reciting يَا قَادِرُ while making Wuḍū?

Answer: The onc who recites يَا قَادِرُ during Wuḍū, will not be kidnapped by his enemy.

Sins fall during Wudu

The Holy Prophet صَلَّى اللهُ تَعَالٰى عَلَيۡهِ وَاٰلِهٖ وَسَلَّم has stated: When a person makes Wuḍū, his sins fall, those of hands when washing hands, those of face whilst washing the face, those of head whilst passing wet hands over the head and those of feet whilst washing the feet. *(Al-Musnad Imām Aḥmad, bin Ḥanbal, Al-Ḥadīš 415, Vol. 1, p.130)*

Ṣalāĥ

Question 1: Should children also offer Ṣalāĥ?

Answer: Yes, children should also offer Ṣalāĥ.

Question 2: How many preconditions of Ṣalāĥ are there?

Answer: There are 6 preconditions of Ṣalāĥ.

Question 3: How many Farāiḍ of Ṣalāĥ are there?

Answer: There are 7 Farāiḍ of Ṣalāĥ.

Question 4: How many and which types of Rak'āt are there in Ṣalat-ul-Fajr?

Answer: There are 4 Rak'āt in Ṣalat-ul-Fajr: 2 Sunnat-e-Muakkadaĥ and 2 Farḍ.

Question 5: How many and which types of Rak'āt are there in Ṣalat-uz-Ẓuĥr?

Answer: There are 12 Rak'āt in Ṣalat-uz- Ẓuĥr: 4 Sunnat-e-Muakkadaĥ, 4 Farḍ, 2 Sunnat-e-Muakkadaĥ and 2 Nafl.

Question 6: How many and which types of Rak'āt are there in Ṣalat-ul-'Aṣr?

Answer: There are 8 Rak'āt in Ṣalat-ul-'Aṣr: 4 Sunnat-e-Ghayr Muakkadaĥ and 4 Farḍ.

Question 7: How many and which types of Rak'āt are there in Ṣalat-ul-Maghrib?

Answer: There are 7 Rak'āt in Ṣalat-ul-Maghrib: 3 Farḍ, 2 Sunnat-e-Muakkadaĥ and 2 Nafl.

Question 8: How many and which types of Rak'āt are there in Ṣalat-ul-'Isha?

Answer: There are 17 Rak'āt in Ṣalat-ul-'Isha: 4 Sunnat-e-Ghayr Muakkadaĥ, 4 Farḍ, 2 Sunnat-e-Muakkadaĥ, 2 Nafl, 3 Witr and 2 Nafl.

Good intentions

12 Good intentions for the recitation of the Holy Quran

1. I will learn the Holy Quran with the intention of gaining the pleasure of Allah عَزَّوَجَلَّ and reward.

2. I will respect the Madanī Qāidaĥ and the Holy Quran.

3. Obeying the Quranic commandment, I will touch the Madanī Qāidaĥ and verses of the Holy Quran with Wuḍū.

4. I will kiss the Madanī Qāidaĥ and the Holy Quran with the intention of reverence.

5. I will make a routine of reciting it at home also.

6. For the pleasure of Allah عَزَّوَجَلَّ, I will always recite it slowly with correct pronunciation of letters.

7 I will donate the reward of recitation of the Madanī Qāidaĥ and the Holy Quran to my kind Murshid, teachers, parents and the entire Ummaĥ of the Beloved Prophet صَلَّى اللّٰهُ تَعَالٰى عَلَيْهِ وَاٰلِهٖ وَسَلَّم.

8 I will obey the commandments of the Holy Quran throughout my life.

9 I will not put unnecessary marks on the Madanī Qāidaĥ and the Holy Quran.

10 I will take care that the pages of the Madanī Qāidaĥ and the Holy Quran will neither tear nor come off the binding.

11 I will keep the Madanī Qāidaĥ and the Holy Quran in a cover to protect them from dust.

12 (Acting upon the Sunnaĥ of keeping the gaze down) I will avoid looking here and there while reciting the Holy Quran, اِنْ شَآءَ اللّٰه عَزَّوَجَلَّ.

Forgiveness of sins by acquisition of knowledge

The Beloved and Blessed Prophet صَلَّى اللّٰهُ تَعَالٰى عَلَيْهِ وَاٰلِهٖ وَسَلَّم has stated, 'The one who wears shoes or socks or clothes [so that he would depart to acquire religious knowledge having worn them] his sins are forgiven as he steps out of his house.' *(Al-Mu'jam-ul-Awsaṭ, Vol. 4, p. 204, Ḥadīš 5722)*

Madina Madina Hamara Madina

Madīnaĥ Madīnaĥ ĥamārā Madīnaĥ
Ĥamayn jān-o-dil say ĥay piyārā Madīnaĥ

Suĥānā suĥānā dil āra Madīnaĥ
Dīwānaun kī ānkĥaun kā tārā Madīnaĥ

Yeĥ ĥar 'Āshiq-e-Mustafa keĥ raĥā ĥay
Ĥamayn tau ĥay Jannat say piyārā Madīnaĥ

Waĥān piyārā Ka'baĥ yaĥān Sabz Gumbad
Woĥ Makkaĥ bĥī mīṫĥā tau piyārā Madīnaĥ

Bulā lī-jiyay apnay qadmaun mayn Āqā
Dikĥā dī-jiyay ab tau piyārā Madīnaĥ

Pĥirūn gird Ka'baĥ piyūn Āb-e-Zam Zam
Mayn pĥir ā kay daykĥūn tumĥārā Madīnaĥ

Khudā gar qiyāmat mayn farmāye māngo
Lagāyain gey dīwānay na'raĥ Madīnaĥ

Madīnay mayn Āqā ĥamayn maut āye
Banay kāsh! Madfan ĥamārā Madīnaĥ

Ḍiyā Pīr-o-Murshid kay Ṣadaqay mayn Āqā
Yeĥ 'Aṭṭār āye do-bāraĥ Madīnaĥ

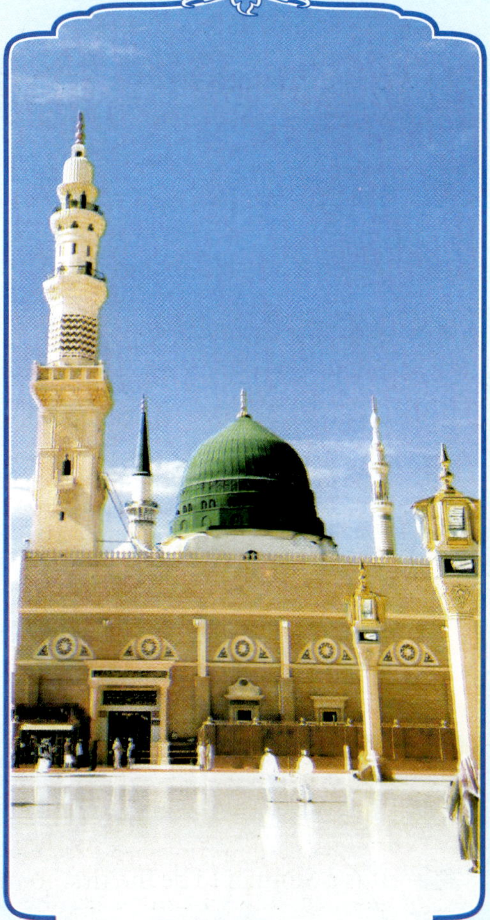

(Wasāil-e-Bakhshish, pp. 187)

Madanī pearls

The Holy Prophet صَلَّى اللهُ تَعَالٰى عَلَيْهِ وَاٰلِهٖ وَسَلَّم has stated: Whoever loved my Sunnaĥ loved me and whoever loved me will be with me in Paradise. *(Mishkāt-ul-Maṣābīḥ, Vol. 1, p. 55, Ḥadīš 175)*

Madanī pearls of making Salām

- We should make Salām to every Muslim.
- When a Muslim makes Salām to us, we should reply to it.
- The best words of Salām are:

  اَلسَّلَامُ عَلَيْكُمْ وَرَحْمَةُ اللهِ وَبَرَكَاتُه

- The best words of the reply to Salām are:

  وَعَلَيْكُمُ السَّلَامُ وَرَحْمَةُ اللهِ وَبَرَكَاتُه

- Ninety mercies descend on the person who makes Salām first and 10 on the one who replies to the Salām. *(Al-Jāmi'-uṣ-Ṣaghīr, Ḥadīš 4870, Mulakhkhaṣān)*
- Salām should be made in a fairly loud voice.
- It is Wājib (necessary) to reply to the Salām immediately.
- It is a Sunnaĥ to be the first to make Salām.
- The younger should make Salām to the elder.
- It is a Sunnaĥ to make Salām while one is entering or leaving the house.
- One should make Salām every time he meets anyone.

Madanī pearls of drinking water

- One should drink water while sitting.
- One should see water in light before he drinks it.
- One should drink water with the right hand.
- One should drink water whilst his head is covered.
- One should recite بِسْمِ اللّٰهِ الرَّحْمٰنِ الرَّحِيْمِ before he drinks water.
- One should recite اَلْحَمْدُ لِلّٰهِ رَبِّ الْعٰلَمِيْنَ after he has drunk water.
- One should drink water in 3 breaths.
- One should drink water slowly with both lips touching the glass.
- One should take care that water should neither fall nor drip whilst he is drinking it.
- Leftover water should not be thrown away.

Madanī pearls of eating food

- It is a Sunnaĥ to wash both hands up to the wrists before and after the eating. *(Sunan Ibn-e-Mājaĥ, Kitāb-ul-Aṭ'imaĥ, Vol. 4, p. 9, Ḥadīš 3260)* Rinse and wash the mouth as well.
- One should eat food whilst sitting according to Sunnaĥ. A Sunnaĥ of sitting whilst eating is to keep the left leg folded on the ground so that the thigh rests on the calf and the right knee is erect. *(Baĥār-e-Sharī'at, Part. 16, p. 21)*
- One should eat food with 3 fingers of the right hand (the thumb, the forefinger and the middle one). *(Mirqāt, Kitāb-ul-Aṭ'imaĥ, Vol. 8, p. 8)*

- It is a Sunnaĥ to recite بِسْمِ اللهِ الرَّحْمٰنِ الرَّحِيْمِ before eating food. *(Ṣaḥīḥ Muslim, Kitāb-ul-Sharī'aĥ, p. 1116, Ḥadīš 20170)*
- One should eat small morsels chewing them properly.
- One should wipe the plate etc. clean after one has finished.
- One should recite اَلْحَمْدُ لِلّٰهِ رَبِّ الْعٰلَمِيْنَ after one has finished.
- If one forgets to recite بِسْمِ اللّٰه or Du'ā in the beginning, one should recite بِسْمِ اللّٰهِ اَوَّلَهٗ وَاٰخِرَه when he recalls it. *(Sunan Abī Dāwūd, Kitāb-ul-Aṭ'imaĥ, Vol. 3, p. 487, Ḥadīš 37667)*
- Break the loaf with the right hand whilst holding it in the left hand.
- Do not take extra food in your plate etc., and take care that it should not fall.
- If rice or crumbs of bread have fallen down, pick them up and eat them as there are tidings of forgiveness for the one doing so.
- Wash and dry your hands properly after you have finished.

Madanī pearls of sneezing

- While sneezing, keep your head downwards and cover your mouth. Voice should be quiet.
- It is a Sunnaĥ to recite اَلْحَمْدُ لِلّٰه after sneezing.
- It is Wājib for the hearer to recite يَرْحَمُكَ الله.
- When the sneezing person listens to the reply of the hearer, he should recite يَغْفِرُ اللهُ لَنَا وَلَكُمْ.

Madanī pearls of yawning

- It is stated in a Ḥadiš, 'When a person yawns, Satan laughs.' *(Ṣaḥīḥ Bukhārī, Kitāb Al-Adab, Vol. 4, p. 163, Ḥadīš 6226)*
- Yawning is from Satan; one should stifle it as much as possible. *(Al-Marja' Al-Sābiq)*
- While yawning, cover your mouth with the back of your left hand.
- A tried and trusted way of stopping yawn is to imagine in the heart that the Prophets عَلَيْهِمُ السَّلَام never yawned. *(Bahār-e-Sharī'at, Vol. 1, p. 538, part. 2)*

Madanī pearls of trimming nails

- Long nails are a seat of Satan. That is, Satan sits on them. *(Kīmiyā-e-Sadat, Vol. 1, p. 168)*
- Biting nails is Makruĥ and can cause leukoderma. *(Rad-ul-Muḥtār, Vol. 9, p. 668)*
- Start trimming nails from the forefinger of the right hand and carry on trimming in sequence until the nail of the little finger gets trimmed, leaving the thumb.
- Then start from the little finger of the left hand and carry on trimming until the nail of the thumb gets trimmed in sequence.
- In the end, trim the nail of the right hand's thumb.

Ethics

Good and Bad Deeds

- Always treat your parents and elders with respect.
- It is rude to talk with parents aloud.
- When parents come, stand up in their honour.
- Kiss your father's hand and mother's foot at least once a day.
- Whole-heartedly do every permissible chore given to you by your parents.
- Make Du'ā for your parents, Murshid and teachers after every Ṣalāĥ.
- Lying is a very grave sin.
- Calling someone names is impermissible and a sin.
- Stealing is also a grave sin.
- Causing harm to any Muslim is a sin.
- Laughing and making noises in Masjid are both forbidden.
- Backbiting is a Ḥarām act leading to Hell.
- Tale-teller will not enter Paradise.
- The one who remained silent got salvation.

Madanī Months

Names of Islamic months

Question 1: How many Madanī (Islamic) months are there?

Answer: There are twelve Madanī (Islamic) months:

- Muḥarram-ul-Ḥarām
- Ṣafar-ul-Muẓaffar
- Rabī'-ul-Awwal (Rabī'-un-Nūr)
- Rabī'-ul-Ākhir (Rabī'-ul-Ghauš)
- Jumādal Awwal
- Jumādal Ukhrā
- Rajab-ul-Murajjab
- Sha'bān-ul-Mu'aẓẓam
- Ramaḍān-ul-Mubārak
- Shawwāl-ul-Mukarram
- Żul-Qa'daĥ-tul-Ḥarām
- Żul-Ḥajjaĥ-tul-Ḥarām

Da'wat-e-Islāmī

Basic Information

Question 1: Tell the name of a global and non-political movement for the preaching of Quran and Sunnaĥ.

Answer: Dawat-e-Islami

Question 2: Tell the name of the founder of Dawat-e-Islami.

Answer: Amīr-e-Aĥl-e-Sunnat 'Allāmaĥ Maulānā Abu Bilal Muhammad Ilyas Attar Qadiri Razavi دَامَتۡ بَرَكَاتُهُمُ الۡعَالِيَه.

Question 3: What is the Madanī aim of Dawat-e-Islami?

Answer: The Madanī aim of Dawat-e-Islami is: 'I must strive to reform myself and the people of the entire world, اِنۡ شَآءَاللّٰه عَزَّوَجَلَّ.'

Question 4: What is the name of the global Madanī Markaz of Dawat-e-Islami and where is it situated?

Answer: The name of the global Madanī Markaz of Dawat-e-Islami is Faīzān-e-Madina situated in Bāb-ul-Madinaĥ (Karachi, Pakistan).

Question 5: After Quran and Ahadis, which religious book in Urdu language is read the most?

Answer: According to an approximation, the most read Islamic book in Urdu language after Quran and Ahadis is Faīzān-e-Sunnat. اَلۡحَمۡدُلِلّٰه عَزَّوَجَلَّ It is a world-famous book and has been translated in English, Hindi, Gujrati, Sindhi and Bangla languages.

Question 6: Who is the author of Faīzān-e-Sunnat?

Answer: Shaykh-e-Tarīqat Amīr-e-Aĥl-e-Sunnat founder of Dawat-e-Islami 'Allāmaĥ Maulānā Abu Bilal Muhammad Ilyas Attar Qadiri Razavi دَامَتۡ بَرَكَاتُهُمُ الۡعَالِيَه.

Manqabat-e-'Aṭṭār

'Aṭṭārī hūn 'Aṭṭārī

Terā karam ĥay Żāt-e-bārī 'Aṭṭārī ĥūn 'Aṭṭārī
Nisbat kiyā ĥay piyārī piyārī 'Aṭṭārī ĥūn 'Aṭṭārī

Āqā day do bayqarārī 'Aṭṭārī ĥūn 'Aṭṭārī
Kartā raĥūn mayn ashk bārī 'Aṭṭārī ĥūn 'Aṭṭārī

Āqā sun lo 'arz ĥamārī 'Aṭṭārī ĥūn 'Aṭṭārī
Pūrī karūn mayn żimmaĥdārī 'Aṭṭārī ĥūn 'Aṭṭārī

Āqā teray sadqay wārī 'Aṭṭārī ĥūn 'Aṭṭārī
Nāzān ĥūn nisbat pay ĥamārī 'Aṭṭārī ĥūn 'Aṭṭārī

Mayn ĥūn Ḍīyāyī mayn ĥūn Raḍawī Sag ĥūn Ghauš-e-Pāk kā
Qādrī ĥūn Qādrī 'Aṭṭārī ĥūn 'Aṭṭārī

Dars-o-bayān say kiyūn gĥabrāun kaysā darr kiyā khauf ĥo
Kiyūn ĥo kisī kā rau'b ṭārī 'Aṭṭārī ĥūn 'Aṭṭārī

Daytā raĥūn naykī kī da'wat chaĥta ĥūn istiqāmat
Guzray yūn hī 'umr sārī 'Aṭṭārī ĥūn 'Aṭṭārī

Piyāray Āqā bakhshwānā Nār-e-Dauzakh say bachānā
'Iṣyān kā ĥay bojĥ bĥārī 'Aṭṭārī ĥūn 'Aṭṭārī

Mayn bĥī daykĥūn Makkaĥ Madīnaĥ Murshid terī ānkĥaun say
Kab āye gī mayrī bārī 'Aṭṭārī ĥūn 'Aṭṭārī

Rauḍa-e-aqdas mimbar nūr mayn bĥī dekĥūn kāsh! Ḥuḍūr
Piyārī dikĥā Jannat kī kīyārī 'Aṭṭārī ĥūn 'Aṭṭārī

Mīṫĥay Murshid mīṫĥā Ḥaram ĥo Maulā ab to aysā karam ĥo
Ḥasrat niklay pĥir to ĥamārī 'Aṭṭārī ĥūn 'Aṭṭārī

Meray Bāpā meray Dātā bĥar do mayrā bĥī tum kāsaĥ
Fayḍ tayrā ĥay jag pay jārī 'Aṭṭārī ĥūn 'Aṭṭārī

Dīd-o-Murshid Qufl-e-Madīnaĥ Bāpā 'aṭā ĥo Fikr-e-Madīnaĥ
Mayn ĥūn mangtā mayn ĥūn bĥikārī 'Aṭṭārī ĥūn 'Aṭṭārī

Express Thanks

The Holy Prophet صَلَّى اللهُ تَعَالٰى عَلَيْهِ وَاٰلِهٖ وَسَلَّم has stated, 'One who has not expressed thanks to people has not expressed gratitude to Allah عَزَّوَجَلَّ.' *(Sunan-ut-Tirmiżī, Kitāb-ul-Bar-e-Waṣilat Vol. 3, p. 384, Ḥadīš 1962)*

Invocations

1 تَسْبِيحِ فَاطِمَه

Recite سُبْحٰنَ اللّٰہِ 33 times, اَلْحَمْدُلِلّٰہِ 33 times and اَللّٰہُ اَکْبَرُ 34 times after every Ṣalāĥ.

2 يَا سَلَامُ

Recite it 111 times and blow on the patient. He will be cured, اِنْ شَآءَاللّٰہ عَزَّوَجَلَّ.

3 يَا وَهَّابُ

Whoever recites it 7 times daily, every Du'ā of his will be fulfilled.

4 يَا عَظِيمُ

Recite it 7 times, blow on water and then drink the water. This will relieve stomach pain, اِنْ شَآءَاللّٰہ عَزَّوَجَلَّ.

5 يَا مُجِيْبُ

Recite it 3 times and blow on the one suffering from headache, his headache will be relieved, اِنْ شَآءَاللّٰہ عَزَّوَجَلَّ.

6 يَا قَوِيُّ

Recite it after the five Farḍ Ṣalāĥ placing your right hand over your head, your memory will improve, اِنْ شَآءَاللّٰہ عَزَّوَجَلَّ.

Ṣalat-'Alan-Nabī ﷺ

صَلَّى اللّٰهُ عَلٰى مُحَمَّد

Seventy doors of mercy are opened for the one who recites this Ṣalat-'Alan-Nabī.

(Al-Qaul Al-Badī', p. 277)

اَللّٰهُمَّ اَنْزِلْهُ الْمَقْعَدَ الْمُقَرَّبَ عِنْدَكَ يَوْمَ الْقِيَامَةِ

The Beloved and Blessed Prophet صَلَّى اللّٰهُ تَعَالٰى عَلَيْهِ وَاٰلِهٖ وَسَلَّم has stated, 'My intercession will become Wājib for the one who recites this Ṣalat.'

(Al-Mu'jam az Zawāid, Vol. 10, p. 254, Ḥadīš 17304; Musnad Imām Aḥmad, bin Ḥanbal, Vol. 6, p. 46, Ḥadīš 16988)

Manqabat Ghauš-e-A'ẓam رَحْمَةُ اللهِ تَعَالٰی عَلَیْه

Asīraun kay Mushkil Kushā Ghauš-e-A'ẓam رَحْمَةُ اللهِ تَعَالٰی عَلَیْه

Asīron kay Mushkil kushā Ghauš-e-A'ẓam
Faqīraun kay Ḥājat-rawā Ghauš-e-A'ẓam

Gĥirā ĥay balāun may bandaĥ tumĥārā
Madad kay liay āo Yā Ghauš-e-A'ẓam

Teray ĥāth mayn ĥāth mayn nay diyā ĥay
Teray ĥāth ĥay lāj Yā Ghauš-e-A'ẓam

Murīdaun ko khatraĥ naĥī baḥr-e-gham say
Kay bayřay kay ĥayn Nā-Khudā Ghauš-e-A'ẓam

Zamānay kay dukh dard kī ranj-o-gham kī
Teray ĥāth may ĥay dawā Ghauš-e-A'ẓam

Nikālā ĥay peĥlay to dūbay ĥūaun ko
Aur ab dūbtaun ko bachā Ghauš-e-A'ẓam

Mayrī mushkilaun ko bĥī āsan kījīay
Kay ĥayn āp Mushkil Kushā Ghauš-e-A'ẓam

Kĥilā day jo murjĥāyi kaliyān dilaun kī
Chalā koyī aysī ĥawā Ghauš-e-A'ẓam

Kaĥay kis say ja kar Ḥasan apnay dil kī
Sunay kaun teray siwā Ghauš-e-A'ẓam

(Żauq-e-Na'at, pp. 124-128)

Munājāt

Maḥabbat mayn apnī gumā Yā Ilāĥī عَزَّوَجَلَّ

Maḥabbat mayn apnī gumā Yā Ilāĥī
Nā pāūn mayn apnā patā Yā Ilāĥī

Raĥūn mast-o-baykhud mayn tayrī wilā mayn
Pilā jām aysā pilā Yā Ilāĥī

Mayn baykār bātaun say bach kar ĥamayshaĥ
Karūn tayrī Ḥamd-o-Sanā Yā Ilāĥī

Mayray ashk beĥtay raĥayn kāsh ĥar dam
Tayray khauf say Yā Khudā Yā Ilāĥī

Gunāĥaun nay mayrī kamar tauř dālī
Mayrā ḥashar mayn hogā kiyā Yā Ilāĥī

Banā day mujĥay nayk naykaun ka sadqaĥ
Gunāĥaun say ĥar dam bachā Yā Ilāĥī

Mayrā ĥar 'amal bas tayray wāsṭay ĥo
Kar ikhlāṣ aysā 'aṭā Yā Ilāĥī

'Ibādat mayn guzray mayrī zindagānī
Karam ĥo karam Yā Khudā Yā Ilāĥī

Musalmān ĥay 'Attar tayrī 'aṭā say
Ĥo īmān par khatimaĥ Yā Ilāĥī

(Wasāil-e-Bakhshish, p. 45)

Ṣalāt-o-Salām

Mustafa Jān-e-Raḥmat pay Lākĥaun Salām

Mustafa Jān-e-Raḥmat pay lākĥaun Salām
Sham'-e-bazm-e-Ĥidāyat pay lākĥaun Salām

Ĥam gharībon kay Āqā pay bay-ḥad Durūd
Ĥam faqīron kī Šarwat pay lākĥaun Salām

Dūr-o-nazdīk kay sun-nay wālay woĥ kān
Kān-e-la'l karāmat pay lākĥaun Salām

Jis kay māthay shafā'at kā Seĥrā raĥā
Us Jabīn-e-Sa'ādat pay lākĥaun Salām

Jis kay sajday ko Miḥrāb-e-Ka'bah jĥukī
Un bĥawaun kī laṭāfat pay lākĥaun Salām

Jis ṭaraf uṫĥ gayī dam mayn dam ā-gayā
Us Nigāĥ-e-'ināyat pay lākĥaun Salām

Patlī patlī gul-e-quds kī pattīyān
Un Labuan kī nazākat pay lākĥaun Salām

Jis kī taskīn say rautay ĥūay ĥans pařay
Us Tabassum kī 'ādat pay lākĥaun Salām

Kul jaĥān milk aur jaw kī rotī ghizā
Us Shikam kī qanā'at pay lākĥaun Salām

Jis sūĥānī gĥaṙī chamkā Ṭaybaĥ ka chānd
Us dil Afrauz-e-Sā'at pay lākĥaun Salām

Ghauš-e-A'ẓam Imāmut-tuqā wannuqā
Jalwaĥ-e-shān-e-qudrat pay lākĥaun Salām

Kāsh Maḥshar mayn jab un kī āmad ĥo aur
Bĥayjayn sab un kī shaukat pay lākĥaun Salām

Mujĥ say khidmat kay qudsī kaĥayn ĥān Raḍā
Mustafa Jān-e-Raḥmat pay lākĥaun Salām

Fayḍ say jin kay lākĥaun 'Imām-e-sajay
Mayray Shaykh-e-Ṭarīqat pay lākĥaun Salām

Jis nay Naykī kī Da'wat ka jazbaĥ diyā
Us Amīr Aĥl-e-Sunnat pay lākĥaun Salām

(Ḥadāiq-e-Bakhshish, pp. 211-229)

Du'ā

Manners of Du'ā

- Express glory to Allah عَزَّوَجَلَّ before you make Du'a: For example, say:

اَلْحَمْدُ لِلّٰهِ رَبِّ الْعٰلَمِيْنَ

- Du'ā is accepted if made with Ṣalāt-'Alan-Nabī before and after it. For example, recite the following:

اَلصَّلٰوةُ وَالسَّلَامُ عَلَيْكَ يَا رَسُوْلَ الله

وَعَلٰى اٰلِكَ وَاَصْحٰبِكَ يَا حَبِيْبَ الله

- Keep your gaze down while making Du'a.
- Looking here and there during Du'ā may cause poor eyesight.
- During Du'a, raise both hands in the straightness of your chest.
- Palms should face the sky during Du'a.

Māšūraĥ Du'a

اَللّٰهُمَّ رَبَّنَآ اٰتِنَا فِى الدُّنْيَا حَسَنَةً وَّفِى
الْاٰخِرَةِ حَسَنَةً وَّقِنَا عَذَابَ النَّارِ

Translation:
O our Rab! Grant us the good of this world and the good of the Hereafter and save us from the torment of the Hell.

اَللّٰهُمَّ رَبِّ زِدْنِىْ عِلْمًا

Translation:
Yā Allah! Enhance my knowledge.

Thanks to a little favour

The Beloved and Blessed Prophet صَلَّى اللّٰهُ تَعَالٰى عَلَيْهِ وَاٰلِهٖ وَسَلَّم has stated, 'The one who has not expressed thanks to a little favour has not also expressed thanks to a greater (favour).'

(Musnad Imām Aḥmad, bin Ḥanbal, Al-Ḥadīš, Vol. 6, p. 394, Ḥadīš 18477)

Bibliography

Al-Jāmi'-uṣ-Ṣaghīr, Imām Jalāluddīn Suyūṭī, Dār-ul-Kutub 'Ilmiyyaĥ, Beirut.

Al-Musnad Imām Aḥmad, Imām Aḥmad Bin Ḥanbal, Dār-ul-Fikr, Beirut.

Al-Qaul-ul-Badī', Imām Ḥāfiẓ Muhammad Bin Sakhāwī, Muwassasa-tul-Riyān.

Baĥār-e-Sharī'at, Muftī Muhammad Amjad 'Alī A'ẓamī, Ziyā-ul-Quran, Publisher, Lahore.

Ḥadāiq-e-Bakhshish, Ala Haḍrat Imām Aḥmad Razā Khān, Maktaba-tul-Madina, Karachi.

Kīmiyā-e-Sa'ādat, Imām Muhammad Bin Muhammad Ghazālī

Majma'-uz-Zawāid, Imām Nūruddīn Ĥayshamī, Dār-ul-Fikr, Beirut.

Mirāt-ul-Manājīḥ, Muftī Aḥmad Yār Khān Na'īmī, Dār-ul-Fikr, Beirut.

Mishkāt-ul-Maṣābīḥ, Imām Muhammad Bin 'Abdullāĥ Khaṭīb, Karachi.

Namāz kay Aḥkām, Amir-e-Aĥl-e-Sunnat, 'Allāmaĥ Maulānā Muhammad Ilyas Attar Qadiri, Maktaba-tul-Madina, Karachi.

Quran Majīd, Ziyā-ul-Quran, Publisher, Lahore

Rad-dul-Muḥtār, 'Allāmaĥ Ibn 'Ābidīn Amīn Shāmī, Dār-ul-Ma'rifaĥ, Beirut.

Ṣaḥīḥ Bukhārī, Imām Muhammad Bin Ismā'īl Bukhārī, Dār-ul-Fikr, Beirut.

Ṣaḥīḥ Muslim, Imām Muslim Bin Ḥajjāj Nayshāpūrī, Dār Ibn Ḥazm, Beirut.

Sunan Abī Dāwūd, Imām Sulaymān Bin Ash'aš, Dār Iḥyā-ut-Turāš-ul-'Arabī, Beirut.

Sunan Ibn-e-Mājaĥ, Imām Muhammad Bin Yazīd Ibn Mājaĥ, Dār-ul-Ma'rifaĥ, Beirut.

Wasāil-e-*Bakhshish*, Amir-e-Aĥl-e-Sunnat, 'Allāmaĥ Maulānā Muhammad Ilyas Attar Qadiri, Maktaba-tul-Madina, Karachi.

Żauq-e-Na'at, Maulānā Ḥassan Razā Khān

Table of Contents